PRINCEWILL LAGANG

# The Digital Nomad Entrepreneur: Freedom in the New Economy

*First published by PRINCEWILL LAGANG 2023*

*Copyright © 2023 by Princewill Lagang*

*All rights reserved. No part of this publication may be reproduced, stored or transmitted in any form or by any means, electronic, mechanical, photocopying, recording, scanning, or otherwise without written permission from the publisher. It is illegal to copy this book, post it to a website, or distribute it by any other means without permission.*

*Princewill Lagang asserts the moral right to be identified as the author of this work.*

*First edition*

*This book was professionally typeset on Reedsy. Find out more at reedsy.com*

# Contents

1 The Digital Nomad Entrepreneur: Freedom in the New Economy  1
2 The Digital Nomad Lifestyle: Benefits and Challenges  4
3 Building a Digital Nomad Business: From Idea to Execution  8
4 Managing Your Digital Nomad Business on the Road  12
5 Financial Management for Digital Nomad Entrepreneurs  16
6 Work-Life Balance and Well-Being for Digital Nomad...  20
7 Remote Team Management for Digital Nomad Entrepreneurs  24
8 Adapting to New Environments and Cultures as a Digital Nomad...  28
9 Personal Growth and Development for Digital Nomad...  32
10 Navigating Challenges and Maintaining Well-Being  36
11 Creating a Sustainable Digital Nomad Lifestyle  40
12 Future-Proofing Your Digital Nomad Lifestyle  44

# 1

# The Digital Nomad Entrepreneur: Freedom in the New Economy

In an ever-evolving world, where technology continues to reshape our lives and redefine traditional norms, a new breed of entrepreneur is emerging – the digital nomad. These individuals have harnessed the power of the internet to create businesses that grant them the ultimate freedom: the ability to work from anywhere on the planet. They have embraced the dynamic nature of the new economy, and in this chapter, we will explore the concept of the digital nomad entrepreneur, its rise, and the transformative potential it holds for those who dare to embrace it.

The Birth of the Digital Nomad

As the early 21st century progressed, a convergence of factors set the stage for the birth of the digital nomad entrepreneur. The widespread availability of high-speed internet, the proliferation of smartphones and portable devices, and the rise of remote work opportunities laid the groundwork for individuals to take their work on the road. Aided by an ever-expanding gig economy, it became increasingly feasible to earn a living while unshackling oneself from a traditional office space.

The term "digital nomad" came into prominence as a way to describe these pioneers. It refers to individuals who leverage digital technology to work remotely, often traveling from one location to another, pursuing their careers while exploring the world. This newfound lifestyle is characterized by the freedom to set one's own schedule, to choose where and when to work, and to adapt to various cultures and environments.

The Entrepreneurial Spirit

Many digital nomads are not just remote workers; they are also entrepreneurs. They have seen the opportunities presented by the digital landscape and have seized them with creativity and determination. These individuals have founded startups, developed online businesses, and created their own paths to financial independence.

The digital nomad entrepreneur embodies the spirit of innovation and adaptability. They are often self-starters who have discovered niche markets and innovative solutions. Whether it's building e-commerce stores, providing freelance services, creating digital content, or offering online courses, their endeavors span a wide array of industries. The digital nomad entrepreneur is not bound by traditional business hours, office politics, or geographical constraints. They operate in a world where ideas and execution are more valuable than physical presence, and success is defined by results, not appearances.

Freedom in the New Economy

The appeal of the digital nomad entrepreneur's lifestyle is undeniable. They enjoy a level of freedom that transcends the boundaries of a 9-to-5 job. In the new economy, success is measured not only in monetary terms but also in terms of personal satisfaction, exploration, and a balanced work-life

# 2

# The Digital Nomad Lifestyle: Benefits and Challenges

In the previous chapter, we introduced the concept of the digital nomad entrepreneur and explored the origins of this innovative lifestyle. Now, we will delve deeper into the digital nomad lifestyle itself, examining the numerous benefits it offers, as well as the unique challenges that come with it.

The Allure of the Digital Nomad Lifestyle

1. Geographic Freedom

One of the most enticing aspects of the digital nomad lifestyle is the ability to work from anywhere in the world. Whether it's a bustling metropolis, a serene beach, or a cozy mountain cabin, digital nomads have the freedom to choose their work environment. This geographic flexibility allows for exploration, cultural immersion, and a deeper appreciation of the world's diversity.

integration. These individuals can choose to work from a tropical beach, a bustling city, or a tranquil mountain retreat, all while staying connected to a global network of clients, customers, and collaborators.

Yet, with this freedom comes the responsibility of managing one's time, finances, and work-life balance. The life of a digital nomad entrepreneur is not without its challenges. We will explore the obstacles and strategies for overcoming them in the chapters to come.

Conclusion

The digital nomad entrepreneur represents a new era of business, one that embraces the possibilities of the digital age and redefines what it means to be successful in the modern world. This book will delve deeper into the journey of these innovative individuals, offering insights, strategies, and inspiration for those who aspire to join their ranks or gain a deeper understanding of the transformative potential of the digital nomad lifestyle.

In the following chapters, we will explore the practical aspects of becoming a digital nomad entrepreneur, from setting up a remote business and managing finances to maintaining work-life balance and staying productive on the road. We will also share the stories of real digital nomad entrepreneurs who have turned their dreams into reality, proving that the freedom and success they enjoy are within reach for those who are willing to embrace the new economy with open arms and an entrepreneurial spirit.

## 2. Work-Life Integration

Digital nomads often enjoy a more integrated work-life balance. With the freedom to set their own schedules, they can align their work with their personal lives, allowing for flexibility and reduced stress. This integration can lead to improved overall well-being and mental health.

## 3. Reduced Living Costs

Depending on their choice of location, digital nomads may experience reduced living costs. They can take advantage of lower expenses in countries with a lower cost of living, allowing them to stretch their income further or invest more in their businesses.

## 4. Diverse Cultural Experiences

The digital nomad lifestyle provides opportunities for unique cultural experiences. By living in different countries and immersing themselves in new cultures, digital nomads can broaden their horizons, learn new languages, and gain a more profound understanding of the world.

## 5. Professional Growth

Digital nomads often experience professional growth by adapting to diverse work environments, collaborating with international clients, and tackling challenges with resourcefulness. This dynamic lifestyle encourages personal and professional development.

# The Challenges of the Digital Nomad Lifestyle

## 1. Unpredictable Income

The irregular nature of freelancing, online businesses, and remote work can result in inconsistent income. Digital nomads must carefully manage their finances and plan for fluctuations in revenue.

2. Isolation

While the freedom to choose work environments is a benefit, it can also lead to isolation. Digital nomads may struggle with loneliness, missing the sense of community and regular social interactions that traditional office settings provide.

3. Time Zone Challenges

Collaborating with clients, teams, or customers across different time zones can be challenging. Coordinating meetings and deadlines becomes a juggling act, requiring strong time management skills.

4. Legal and Administrative Hurdles

Navigating the legal and administrative requirements of working and living in multiple countries can be complex. Digital nomads must understand visa regulations, tax obligations, and other legal considerations.

5. Distractions and Productivity

Working from diverse locations can introduce distractions that impact productivity. Digital nomads need to develop effective work habits and discipline to maintain a high level of output.

Strategies for Success

To thrive in the digital nomad lifestyle, individuals must develop strategies to maximize the benefits and overcome the challenges. In the following chapters, we will explore these strategies in detail, providing practical advice on financial management, maintaining work-life balance, managing time zones, and overcoming isolation.

We will also share personal stories and experiences from successful digital nomad entrepreneurs who have mastered the art of balancing the allure of geographic freedom with the demands of entrepreneurship. By learning from their journeys and applying the strategies outlined in this book, you can navigate the digital nomad lifestyle with confidence and achieve the freedom and success that it offers.

# 3

# Building a Digital Nomad Business: From Idea to Execution

In the previous chapters, we explored the concept of the digital nomad entrepreneur and the benefits and challenges of the digital nomad lifestyle. Now, we shift our focus to the practical aspects of building a successful business as a digital nomad. This chapter will guide you through the process of taking your entrepreneurial idea from inception to execution, ensuring that it aligns with the freedom and flexibility that the digital nomad lifestyle offers.

Navigating the Digital Landscape

1. Identifying Your Niche

Successful digital nomad businesses often begin with a clear focus on a niche market. Identifying your niche allows you to tailor your products or services to a specific audience, giving you a competitive edge and a clearer marketing strategy.

## 2. Market Research

Before diving in, conduct thorough market research to understand your target audience's needs, preferences, and pain points. This information will help you refine your business concept and develop offerings that resonate with potential customers.

## 3. Online Presence

Establishing a strong online presence is essential for a digital nomad business. Create a professional website, set up social media profiles, and ensure your online branding is consistent and compelling. Your digital footprint is often the first point of contact with potential clients.

## Business Models for Digital Nomads

## 1. Freelancing

Many digital nomads start by offering freelance services in their areas of expertise. Common freelance roles include copywriting, web development, graphic design, digital marketing, and consulting. Freelancing provides flexibility and quick income opportunities.

## 2. E-commerce

E-commerce businesses involve selling physical or digital products online. This could include dropshipping, print-on-demand, handmade goods, or digital downloads. Running an e-commerce business allows you to generate passive income and manage operations remotely.

## 3. Digital Products and Services

Creating and selling digital products and services, such as online courses, e-books, software, or design templates, is a scalable business model. Once created, these products can generate recurring income with minimal ongoing effort.

4. Remote Consulting and Coaching

Leveraging your expertise to provide remote consulting or coaching services can be a lucrative digital nomad business. This model often involves one-on-one or group sessions and allows for a flexible schedule.

Developing a Business Plan

A well-thought-out business plan is a crucial tool for any digital nomad entrepreneur. Your business plan should outline your business goals, target market, marketing strategy, revenue projections, and a clear action plan. It serves as a roadmap to keep you on track and make informed decisions.

Legal Considerations and Taxes

Understanding the legal requirements and tax implications of your digital nomad business is essential. Depending on your location and the nature of your business, you may need to register your business, obtain necessary licenses, and comply with tax regulations in different countries.

Managing Finances

Effective financial management is a key aspect of running a successful digital nomad business. Budgeting, tracking expenses, and setting financial goals are critical to maintain financial stability while pursuing the nomadic lifestyle.

Conclusion

In this chapter, we've laid the foundation for building a digital nomad business.

From choosing your niche and developing a business plan to understanding the legal and financial aspects, you're now equipped with the knowledge to start your entrepreneurial journey. The next chapters will delve deeper into the practicalities of maintaining your business on the road, managing your work-life balance, and thriving as a digital nomad entrepreneur.

# 4

# Managing Your Digital Nomad Business on the Road

Now that you've explored the concept of the digital nomad entrepreneur and have laid the groundwork for your business, it's time to dive into the practical aspects of managing your business while embracing the nomadic lifestyle. In this chapter, we'll discuss strategies for maintaining a successful digital nomad business, handling the challenges of remote work, and ensuring you stay productive and motivated on the road.

Creating a Portable Office

1. Choose the Right Tools

Selecting the right set of tools and software is crucial to your success as a digital nomad. Invest in a reliable laptop, mobile devices, and high-quality internet connections. Consider cloud-based productivity tools and project management software to keep your work organized and accessible from anywhere.

## 2. Ergonomic Work Setup

Pay attention to your physical workspace. Ensure that your workspace is comfortable and ergonomically designed, whether you're working at a co-working space, a cafe, or your accommodation. An ergonomic chair and an adjustable desk can make a significant difference in your work quality and well-being.

## Time Management and Productivity

### 1. Establish a Routine

Creating a daily routine helps you maintain productivity and a sense of structure. Allocate specific time slots for work, exercise, relaxation, and exploration. Consistency in your routine is essential for work-life balance.

### 2. Avoid Overwork

It's easy for digital nomads to overwork, given the flexibility of their schedule. Set clear boundaries and stick to them. Overworking can lead to burnout, which is detrimental to both your business and personal life.

### 3. Goal Setting

Set clear, achievable goals for your business and personal life. Having objectives to work towards gives you a sense of purpose and motivation. Break larger goals into smaller, actionable tasks to track progress.

### 4. Time Zone Management

If your business involves clients or team members in different time zones, mastering time zone management is critical. Use scheduling tools to coordinate meetings and deadlines effectively. Communicate your availability and expectations clearly.

Staying Connected

1. Network Building

Networking is crucial for any business, and it's equally important for digital nomads. Attend industry events, join online communities, and connect with fellow nomads and potential clients. Building a strong network can open up new opportunities and collaborations.

2. Communication

Clear and effective communication is key when working remotely. Choose communication tools that suit your needs, such as video conferencing, instant messaging, or project management platforms. Establish regular check-ins with your team or clients to maintain transparency and alignment.

Coping with Isolation

1. Seek Social Interaction

Combat loneliness and isolation by seeking social interaction. Connect with fellow digital nomads, participate in local events, and make an effort to engage with the local community. Building relationships can enhance your travel experience and mental well-being.

2. Travel Companions

Consider traveling with a partner, friend, or coworker. Having a companion can provide emotional support, share experiences, and reduce feelings of isolation.

## Security and Health

### 1. Data Security

Protect your digital assets and sensitive information by using secure internet connections, strong passwords, and reliable antivirus software. Consider using a virtual private network (VPN) for an extra layer of security.

### 2. Health and Wellness

Prioritize your health by maintaining a balanced diet, regular exercise, and adequate sleep. Access to healthcare while traveling is essential, so ensure you have the necessary health insurance or coverage.

## Conclusion

Managing a digital nomad business comes with its unique set of challenges, but with the right strategies and mindset, you can maintain a successful and fulfilling entrepreneurial journey. In the following chapters, we will explore additional aspects of the digital nomad lifestyle, from financial management and maintaining work-life balance to overcoming challenges specific to remote work and travel. Your digital nomad adventure is well underway, and with the tools and knowledge you're acquiring, you're better prepared to navigate the road ahead.

# 5

# Financial Management for Digital Nomad Entrepreneurs

As a digital nomad entrepreneur, you have embraced a lifestyle that offers freedom and flexibility. However, managing your finances effectively is essential to sustain your entrepreneurial journey and maintain the lifestyle you desire. In this chapter, we will explore strategies and best practices for financial management that will help you achieve your business and personal financial goals while on the road.

Setting a Financial Foundation

1. Create a Budget

Start by creating a detailed budget that outlines your monthly expenses, including accommodation, transportation, food, insurance, and business costs. Understanding your financial commitments is crucial for making informed decisions.

2. Emergency Fund

Building an emergency fund is a fundamental step in financial planning. Having a financial safety net can help you handle unexpected expenses, such as medical emergencies or equipment replacements, without disrupting your business.

Business Finances

1. Separate Business and Personal Accounts

Maintain separate bank accounts for your business and personal finances. This separation simplifies accounting, tracks business expenses, and ensures you can easily identify your business's financial health.

2. Tax Planning

Understand the tax implications of your nomadic lifestyle and business structure. Seek professional advice if necessary to ensure you comply with tax regulations in both your home country and the countries you visit.

3. Invoicing and Payment Processing

Use reliable invoicing and payment processing systems to streamline financial transactions. Choose payment methods that work well for your clients and partners, and consider currency conversion fees if you work internationally.

Managing Income and Expenses

1. Consistent Income Streams

Diversify your income streams to reduce financial risk. Depending solely on one client or revenue source can leave you vulnerable if that source dries up.

2. Tracking Expenses

Regularly track your expenses to stay within your budget. Consider using expense tracking apps or software to simplify the process. Keeping an eye on your spending ensures you don't overspend or accumulate unnecessary debt.

3. Savings and Investments

Set financial goals for saving and investing. Whether you're saving for retirement, a future business expansion, or other financial goals, allocate a portion of your income toward savings and investments.

Currency Exchange and Banking

1. Choose the Right Banking Services

Select a bank or financial service that provides international access, low or no foreign transaction fees, and convenient online banking. Digital nomads often prefer banks that offer multi-currency accounts.

2. Currency Exchange

Stay informed about exchange rates and consider using reliable currency exchange services or apps to minimize fees and get the best rates when transferring money.

Risk Management

1. Insurance

Consider obtaining comprehensive travel and health insurance. Travel insurance can protect you from unexpected travel-related issues, while health insurance ensures you have access to medical care while abroad.

2. Contingency Planning

Prepare for unforeseen circumstances by having contingency plans in place. This might include backup sources of income, a list of trusted contacts for emergencies, and copies of important documents in a secure digital location.

Conclusion

Effective financial management is a cornerstone of a successful digital nomad entrepreneur's journey. By setting a solid financial foundation, managing your business finances, and making informed choices, you can not only sustain your entrepreneurial venture but also enjoy the freedom and flexibility of the digital nomad lifestyle without constant financial stress. In the following chapters, we will continue to explore additional aspects of the digital nomad lifestyle, helping you navigate the challenges and opportunities that come your way.

# 6

# Work-Life Balance and Well-Being for Digital Nomad Entrepreneurs

Balancing work and personal life is a constant challenge, and as a digital nomad entrepreneur, it can be even more demanding. In this chapter, we will explore strategies for maintaining a healthy work-life balance, managing well-being, and finding harmony between your entrepreneurial endeavors and the nomadic lifestyle.

Prioritizing Work-Life Balance

1. Establish Boundaries

Set clear boundaries between work and personal life. Designate specific work hours, and avoid the temptation to continually check emails or work-related tasks during your personal time.

2. Create a Dedicated Workspace

Design a workspace within your accommodation that is separate from your leisure area. Having a defined space for work helps maintain a mental boundary between work and personal life.

3. Schedule Leisure Time

Plan leisure activities, explore your surroundings, and make the most of your travel experiences. Schedule downtime to recharge and prevent burnout.

4. Embrace the "Slow Travel" Approach

Rather than constantly moving from one location to another, consider adopting a "slow travel" approach. Staying in a location for a longer period can reduce travel-related stress and provide a deeper cultural immersion.

Managing Stress and Well-Being

1. Mindfulness and Meditation

Incorporate mindfulness and meditation practices into your daily routine to reduce stress and maintain mental well-being. These practices can help you stay focused and grounded amidst the challenges of the digital nomad lifestyle.

2. Exercise and Diet

Prioritize physical health by maintaining a regular exercise regimen and a balanced diet. Exercise helps alleviate stress, while a nutritious diet ensures you have the energy needed for work and travel.

3. Sleep Hygiene

Establish a healthy sleep routine to ensure you get adequate rest. Create a comfortable sleep environment and avoid excessive use of screens before bedtime.

## Social Connection

### 1. Build Relationships

Actively seek social interaction with fellow digital nomads and locals. Building relationships can provide emotional support, counteract loneliness, and enhance your travel experience.

### 2. Join Digital Nomad Communities

Participate in digital nomad communities, both online and in person. Engaging with like-minded individuals can lead to valuable connections, shared experiences, and opportunities for collaboration.

## Technology Detox

### 1. Unplug Occasionally

Give yourself a technology detox by disconnecting from screens and devices, even if just for a short period each day. This practice can help you recharge and stay present in the moment.

### 2. Limit Notifications

Minimize digital distractions by disabling unnecessary notifications on your devices. This can reduce the constant urge to check messages and emails.

## Embracing Flexibility

### 1. Embrace Spontaneity

One of the advantages of the digital nomad lifestyle is the flexibility it offers. Embrace spontaneity and allow for occasional deviations from your planned schedule.

2. Adapt to Change

Stay open to change and adapt to unexpected challenges. The ability to pivot and adjust to new situations is a valuable skill for digital nomad entrepreneurs.

Conclusion

Maintaining work-life balance and well-being is an ongoing journey for digital nomad entrepreneurs. By establishing boundaries, managing stress, fostering social connections, and embracing the flexibility of your lifestyle, you can enjoy the freedom of being a digital nomad while maintaining your physical and mental well-being.

In the following chapters, we will delve into specific challenges and solutions that digital nomads may encounter, from managing remote teams to dealing with culture shock and adjusting to new environments. Your journey as a digital nomad entrepreneur is a dynamic one, and mastering these aspects will contribute to a fulfilling and sustainable lifestyle.

# 7

# Remote Team Management for Digital Nomad Entrepreneurs

One of the challenges digital nomad entrepreneurs often face is managing remote teams effectively. In this chapter, we will explore strategies for building and leading a remote team that can support your business and enable you to maintain your nomadic lifestyle while achieving your entrepreneurial goals.

The Value of Remote Teams

1. Global Talent Access

Remote teams provide access to a diverse pool of talent from around the world. This diversity can bring fresh perspectives and skills to your business.

2. Scalability

Remote teams allow your business to scale up or down more flexibly as needed. You can adjust your team size and skill sets to accommodate your business's growth or changes.

### 3. Cost Efficiency

Hiring remote team members can often be more cost-effective than maintaining a physical office, as you save on office space and related expenses.

Building a High-Performing Remote Team

### 1. Define Roles and Expectations

Clearly define the roles and responsibilities of each team member. Set expectations for communication, work hours, and deliverables to avoid misunderstandings.

### 2. Effective Onboarding

Provide a comprehensive onboarding process for new team members. This includes training on your business processes, tools, and culture. An efficient onboarding process ensures your remote team is well-prepared and aligned with your business goals.

### 3. Communication Tools

Use reliable communication and collaboration tools to foster effective remote teamwork. Tools like video conferencing, project management software, and instant messaging platforms enable seamless communication and project coordination.

### 4. Regular Meetings

Schedule regular team meetings to ensure alignment and foster a sense of community. These meetings can include updates, brainstorming sessions, and opportunities for team members to connect.

## Leading and Managing a Remote Team

### 1. Trust and Autonomy

Build trust with your team by allowing team members the autonomy to manage their work. Micromanagement can hinder productivity and morale.

### 2. Performance Metrics

Set clear performance metrics and key performance indicators (KPIs) to measure your team's success. Regularly review progress and provide constructive feedback.

### 3. Flexibility

Recognize and accommodate the different time zones and working hours of your team members. Ensure that your team can maintain a healthy work-life balance while working remotely.

## Overcoming Challenges

### 1. Communication Gaps

Effective communication is a constant challenge for remote teams. Be proactive in addressing misunderstandings and ensure that team members have the tools and resources to communicate effectively.

### 2. Isolation

Remote team members may experience feelings of isolation. Encourage team bonding through virtual team-building activities, and create opportunities for social interaction.

3. Cultural Differences

Working with a diverse team can lead to cultural differences and misunderstandings. Foster a culture of respect and sensitivity to different cultural backgrounds.

Conclusion

Managing a remote team as a digital nomad entrepreneur is an essential skill for growing your business and maintaining your nomadic lifestyle. By defining roles, using effective communication tools, providing training, and addressing common challenges, you can build a high-performing remote team that supports your entrepreneurial journey. In the following chapters, we will explore additional aspects of the digital nomad lifestyle and provide insights to help you navigate the unique challenges and opportunities that arise while traveling and running your business.

# 8

# Adapting to New Environments and Cultures as a Digital Nomad Entrepreneur

As a digital nomad entrepreneur, you'll frequently find yourself in new environments and immersed in diverse cultures. Adapting to these changes is essential for both your business and personal well-being. In this chapter, we'll explore strategies for effectively adapting to new environments and cultures while maintaining your entrepreneurial journey.

Embracing Cultural Diversity

1. Cultivate Cultural Sensitivity

To adapt to new environments and cultures, it's crucial to cultivate cultural sensitivity. This involves an understanding and respect for the customs, traditions, and beliefs of the people you encounter.

2. Learn Local Language Basics

While you don't need to become fluent in every language, learning some basic phrases can go a long way in building rapport with locals and enhancing your travel experience.

3. Explore Local Cuisine

Sampling local cuisine is a great way to connect with a new culture. Trying different dishes and dining at local eateries can provide insight into the local way of life.

Navigating Practicalities

1. Transportation

Familiarize yourself with local transportation options. Whether it's public transit, ridesharing services, or renting a bicycle, understanding how to get around in a new environment is vital.

2. Accommodation

Choose accommodations that align with your work and lifestyle needs. Consider factors such as reliable internet access, a comfortable workspace, and proximity to essential amenities.

3. Healthcare

Research healthcare options in your new location. Ensure you have access to medical care and understand how to navigate the local healthcare system, if necessary.

Overcoming Culture Shock

1. Preparing for Culture Shock

Culture shock is a common experience when immersing yourself in a new culture. Understand that it's a natural reaction to the unfamiliar and be prepared to adapt gradually.

2. Stay Open-Minded

Keep an open mind and be patient with yourself as you adjust to new cultural norms. Recognize that different does not necessarily mean wrong or inferior.

3. Seek Support

Connect with fellow digital nomads and local expat communities. Sharing experiences and advice can help you cope with culture shock and adapt more smoothly.

Maintaining Business Amidst Change

1. Flexible Work Arrangements

Ensure your business can adapt to your changing environments. Have the necessary tools and technology to work from various locations without disruptions.

2. Time Management

Maintain a consistent time management strategy that accommodates different time zones and work environments. Set your work hours to align with your most productive times and your clients' schedules.

3. Prioritizing Business Needs

Prioritize your business responsibilities while adapting to new environments. Ensure your business operations are not compromised while exploring new cultures and locales.

## Conclusion

Adapting to new environments and cultures is a fundamental aspect of the digital nomad lifestyle. By developing cultural sensitivity, learning local basics, and mastering practicalities, you can make the most of your travel experiences. Embrace the opportunities for personal and professional growth that come with exploring diverse cultures while running your entrepreneurial venture.

In the following chapters, we will delve into additional facets of the digital nomad lifestyle, including strategies for personal growth, financial success, and work-life balance. Your journey as a digital nomad entrepreneur is multifaceted, and the ability to adapt to new environments and cultures is a valuable skill that will enhance your nomadic experience.

# 9

# Personal Growth and Development for Digital Nomad Entrepreneurs

Beyond business success, the digital nomad lifestyle offers unique opportunities for personal growth and development. In this chapter, we will explore strategies for self-improvement and ways to make the most of your nomadic journey in terms of personal fulfillment and growth.

Embracing the Learning Mindset

1. Lifelong Learning

As a digital nomad entrepreneur, your journey is an ongoing adventure of learning and discovery. Embrace a lifelong learning mindset, staying curious and open to new experiences.

2. Skill Development

Identify skills that can enhance your entrepreneurial journey and personal growth. Whether it's learning a new language, improving your public speaking abilities, or mastering a particular business skill, continuous self-improvement is vital.

Building Resilience

1. Embracing Challenges

The nomadic lifestyle is not without its challenges, and these experiences can be an opportunity for personal growth. Embrace challenges as opportunities to learn and grow, and develop resilience in the face of adversity.

2. Mindfulness and Stress Management

Practice mindfulness and stress management techniques to maintain your mental and emotional well-being. Techniques like meditation, deep breathing, and regular exercise can help you navigate the inevitable ups and downs of the digital nomad journey.

Expanding Your Comfort Zone

1. Try New Experiences

Use your travels as a chance to expand your comfort zone. Whether it's trying a new activity, cuisine, or engaging in an unfamiliar cultural practice, taking risks can lead to personal growth.

2. Facing Cultural Diversity

Interacting with diverse cultures challenges your preconceived notions and broadens your horizons. Engage with locals, immerse yourself in their customs, and seek to understand their perspectives.

Finding a Work-Life Balance

1. Quality of Life

Remember that your quality of life is a crucial part of your journey as a digital nomad entrepreneur. Balance work and personal life, making time for leisure, relaxation, and personal growth.

2. Self-Care

Prioritize self-care by taking care of your physical and mental health. Ensure you get adequate rest, exercise, and nutrition to maintain a healthy and balanced lifestyle.

Personal Goal Setting

1. Define Personal Goals

Set personal goals alongside your business objectives. These goals can be related to travel experiences, personal development, or any area of your life that you wish to improve.

2. Monitor Progress

Regularly review and monitor your progress toward personal goals. Use your entrepreneurial skills in goal setting and execution to achieve personal fulfillment.

Contribution and Giving Back

1. Philanthropy

Consider how you can contribute to the communities and places you visit. Whether through volunteering, supporting local causes, or sharing your knowledge and skills, giving back can be a rewarding part of your journey.

## 2. Environmental Responsibility

As a traveler, be mindful of your environmental impact. Practice responsible and sustainable travel by reducing your carbon footprint and contributing to the conservation of natural and cultural resources.

## Conclusion

The digital nomad lifestyle is not just about business success but also about personal growth, self-discovery, and contributing to the world in meaningful ways. By embracing a learning mindset, building resilience, expanding your comfort zone, and maintaining a work-life balance, you can maximize the personal development opportunities that come with your nomadic journey.

In the following chapters, we will explore additional aspects of the digital nomad lifestyle, from financial management and remote work challenges to maintaining mental and emotional well-being. Your journey as a digital nomad entrepreneur is multifaceted, and the pursuit of personal growth and fulfillment is a fulfilling part of it.

# 10

# Navigating Challenges and Maintaining Well-Being

As a digital nomad entrepreneur, your journey is a dynamic and ever-changing adventure. This chapter will address common challenges faced by digital nomads and provide strategies for maintaining well-being, personal growth, and business success while on the road.

Overcoming Common Challenges

1. Loneliness and Isolation

The nomadic lifestyle can sometimes lead to feelings of loneliness and isolation. To combat these feelings, actively seek social interaction, connect with local communities, and maintain strong relationships with friends and family.

2. Cultural Adjustment

Adapting to different cultures and environments can be challenging. Be patient and open-minded, learn about local customs and traditions, and embrace cultural diversity.

3. Travel Logistics

The logistics of travel, such as transportation, accommodation, and navigating new cities, can be stressful. Plan and research thoroughly, stay organized, and be adaptable in the face of travel hiccups.

4. Internet Connectivity

Reliable internet access is essential for remote work. Invest in mobile hotspots, local SIM cards, and VPNs to ensure you have a stable connection in various locations.

5. Time Management

Balancing work and personal life across different time zones can be a complex task. Maintain a consistent routine, use time management tools, and communicate effectively with your team and clients about your availability.

Managing Remote Work Challenges

1. Overcoming Distractions

Digital nomads often work from diverse and potentially distracting locations. Establish a focused work environment, practice self-discipline, and use productivity techniques to stay on track.

2. Isolation from Colleagues

Remote work can lead to isolation from colleagues and a sense of disconnection from your team. Foster regular communication and virtual team-building activities to maintain a sense of belonging.

3. Boundary Setting

Without a physical office, it's crucial to set boundaries between work and personal life. Designate specific work hours and spaces to ensure you have time for relaxation and leisure.

Maintaining Well-Being

1. Stress Management

Stress is a common aspect of the digital nomad lifestyle. Develop stress management techniques like meditation, exercise, and relaxation to help you cope with the demands of work and travel.

2. Mental Health

Prioritize mental health by seeking support when needed. Digital nomads may experience feelings of anxiety or depression, so be open to talking about your mental health and seeking professional assistance.

3. Physical Health

Maintain physical health by staying active, eating well, and getting adequate sleep. Regular exercise and a balanced diet are essential for energy and well-being.

4. Routine and Structure

Establishing a daily routine provides structure and stability. A routine can help you manage your work, personal life, and well-being, especially in new and unpredictable environments.

## Conclusion

The digital nomad lifestyle is an ever-changing adventure that presents numerous challenges and opportunities for personal and professional growth. By addressing common challenges, practicing effective time management, and prioritizing well-being, you can navigate the complexities of the nomadic journey while maintaining your entrepreneurial success and personal fulfillment.

In the following chapters, we will explore additional facets of the digital nomad lifestyle, from financial management and personal development to work-life balance and overcoming specific challenges. Your journey as a digital nomad entrepreneur is a multifaceted one, and the ability to overcome challenges and maintain well-being is a valuable skill that will enhance your nomadic experience.

# 11

# Creating a Sustainable Digital Nomad Lifestyle

A sustainable digital nomad lifestyle involves balancing the freedom and flexibility of travel with long-term well-being and business success. In this chapter, we will explore strategies for creating a sustainable digital nomad lifestyle that allows you to thrive and continue your journey for the long haul.

Balancing Freedom and Responsibility

1. Set Clear Goals

Define your personal and business goals, including financial, professional, and personal objectives. Having clear goals provides direction and purpose for your nomadic lifestyle.

2. Financial Stability

Achieve financial stability by managing your business finances effectively.

Maintain a financial safety net and plan for contingencies to ensure that you can sustain your lifestyle.

3. Business Sustainability

Ensure the sustainability of your business by diversifying your income streams, managing your remote team, and adapting to market changes. Continuously assess your business's long-term viability.

Sustainable Travel Practices

1. Eco-Friendly Travel

Practice eco-friendly travel by minimizing your environmental impact. Reduce waste, support sustainable tourism, and offset your carbon footprint when possible.

2. Slow Travel

Consider adopting a slow travel approach, spending longer periods in each location to reduce the environmental impact of frequent travel and to gain a deeper understanding of local cultures.

3. Community Engagement

Contribute to the communities you visit by supporting local businesses, volunteering, and participating in community events. Foster positive connections with the places you explore.

Personal Well-Being and Fulfillment

1. Work-Life Balance

Maintain a healthy work-life balance by setting boundaries and prioritizing personal time for relaxation and leisure. Balance is essential for long-term well-being.

2. Mental Health

Prioritize mental health by seeking professional help if needed and practicing mindfulness and stress management. A resilient mindset is crucial for sustainability.

3. Personal Development

Continue to focus on personal development and lifelong learning. Expanding your skills, knowledge, and experiences can lead to greater fulfillment and growth.

Building a Supportive Community

1. Digital Nomad Networks

Engage with digital nomad communities and networks, both online and in person. Sharing experiences, tips, and support with fellow nomads can help you stay motivated and navigate challenges.

2. Mentorship and Coaching

Consider seeking mentorship or coaching from experienced digital nomad entrepreneurs. Learning from their experiences and insights can help you make informed decisions and sustain your lifestyle.

Conclusion

Creating a sustainable digital nomad lifestyle involves finding harmony between your entrepreneurial goals, personal well-being, and the freedom of travel. By balancing freedom and responsibility, adopting eco-friendly travel practices, and focusing on well-being, you can embark on a lifelong journey as a digital nomad entrepreneur.

In the following chapters, we will continue to explore various aspects of the digital nomad lifestyle, providing insights into managing specific challenges, thriving as a remote worker, and achieving your entrepreneurial dreams. Your journey is a dynamic one, and with the right strategies, you can create a sustainable and fulfilling nomadic lifestyle.

# 12

# Future-Proofing Your Digital Nomad Lifestyle

The world is ever-evolving, and as a digital nomad entrepreneur, it's crucial to future-proof your lifestyle and adapt to emerging trends and challenges. In this chapter, we will explore strategies to ensure your digital nomad lifestyle remains relevant and sustainable in the face of change.

Embracing Technological Advancements

1. Stay Current with Technology

Keep up to date with the latest technological advancements and tools relevant to your business and industry. Embracing new technologies can streamline your work and give you a competitive edge.

2. Automation and Artificial Intelligence

Explore automation and artificial intelligence tools to simplify repetitive tasks and enhance your business's efficiency. These technologies can free up your time for more strategic activities.

3. Cybersecurity

With the increasing reliance on digital tools and remote work, prioritize cybersecurity to protect your business and personal data from potential threats and cyberattacks.

Adapting to Changing Work Trends

1. Remote Work Evolution

Stay informed about the evolution of remote work trends. As the remote work landscape changes, adapt your business operations and work practices accordingly.

2. Gig Economy Opportunities

Explore opportunities in the gig economy, which continues to grow. Freelancing, consulting, and short-term projects can be valuable additions to your business model.

3. Continuous Learning

Commit to lifelong learning to adapt to evolving industries and skill requirements. Pursuing additional training and certifications can keep your skills relevant.

Sustainable Travel and Environmental Responsibility

1. Eco-Friendly Practices

As awareness of environmental sustainability increases, maintain eco-friendly travel practices and incorporate sustainability into your lifestyle. This includes minimizing waste, using eco-conscious products, and supporting green businesses.

2. Digital Nomad Hubs

Stay updated on emerging digital nomad hubs and communities. These hubs often provide infrastructure, support, and networking opportunities that can enhance your nomadic experience.

3. Local Involvement

Contribute to the local communities you visit by supporting local businesses and initiatives. Engaging with the local culture and economy can provide a more meaningful travel experience.

Future-Proofing Financial Success

1. Diversification

Continue to diversify your income streams and investments. Diversification provides financial stability and flexibility in times of economic uncertainty.

2. Financial Planning

Regularly assess your financial plan and adapt it to changing circumstances and long-term goals. Seek professional financial advice when necessary to ensure your financial health.

3. Retirement Planning

Plan for retirement as a digital nomad. Consider options for long-term financial security, such as retirement accounts and investments.

Staying Agile and Resilient

1. Adaptability

Cultivate adaptability and a willingness to pivot when necessary. The ability to adapt to changing circumstances is a valuable skill for future-proofing your lifestyle.

2. Resilience

Continue to build resilience in the face of challenges. Resilience will help you overcome setbacks and navigate the uncertainties of the digital nomad lifestyle.

3. Networking and Support

Maintain a strong network of fellow digital nomad entrepreneurs who can provide support, share insights, and collaborate on projects. Networking is a valuable resource in an ever-changing world.

Conclusion

Future-proofing your digital nomad lifestyle involves staying adaptable, informed, and prepared for change. By embracing technological advancements, adapting to changing work trends, promoting sustainability, securing financial success, and cultivating agility and resilience, you can ensure your digital nomad lifestyle remains relevant and sustainable for years to come.

In "The Digital Nomad Entrepreneur: Freedom in the New Economy," we've explored various aspects of the digital nomad lifestyle and how to succeed as an entrepreneur while maintaining the freedom to travel and work from anywhere. Here's a summary of the chapters:

Chapter 1: The Digital Nomad Entrepreneur
 - Introduced the concept of the digital nomad lifestyle.
 - Explored the benefits and challenges of being a digital nomad entrepreneur.
 - Emphasized the importance of freedom, flexibility, and personal fulfillment.

Chapter 2: Starting Your Digital Nomad Journey
 - Covered the initial steps to becoming a digital nomad entrepreneur.
 - Discussed setting goals, planning, and making the necessary preparations.
 - Emphasized the importance of choosing the right business model and niche.

Chapter 3: Building Your Digital Nomad Business
 - Provided insights into building and launching your business while on the road.
 - Discussed branding, marketing, and customer acquisition.
 - Highlighted the advantages of a location-independent business.

Chapter 4: Managing Your Digital Nomad Business on the Road
 - Explored strategies for maintaining a successful business while traveling.
 - Covered creating a portable office, time management, staying connected, and coping with isolation.
 - Addressed security and health concerns.

Chapter 5: Financial Management for Digital Nomad Entrepreneurs
 - Discussed budgeting, emergency funds, and financial stability.
 - Explored business finances, tax planning, and savings and investments.
 - Covered currency exchange, risk management, and sustainability.

Chapter 6: Work-Life Balance and Well-Being

- Addressed the importance of establishing work-life balance and managing well-being.

- Provided strategies for prioritizing leisure, managing stress, and seeking social interaction.

- Emphasized the need for mindfulness and flexibility.

Chapter 7: Remote Team Management

- Focused on managing remote teams effectively as a digital nomad entrepreneur.

- Covered building and leading a remote team, defining roles, and communication.

- Discussed challenges and solutions related to remote team management.

Chapter 8: Adapting to New Environments and Cultures

- Explored strategies for adapting to new environments and cultures while traveling.

- Highlighted the importance of cultural sensitivity and eco-friendly travel practices.

- Addressed practicalities and overcoming culture shock.

Chapter 9: Personal Growth and Development

- Discussed personal growth and development opportunities on the road.

- Emphasized the importance of continuous learning, resilience, and expanding comfort zones.

- Covered well-being, self-care, and contributing to local communities.

Chapter 10: Navigating Challenges and Maintaining Well-Being

- Addressed common challenges faced by digital nomads and provided strategies for well-being.

- Covered challenges like loneliness, cultural adjustment, and stress management.

- Discussed maintaining well-being through personal and mental health, physical health, and routine.

Chapter 11: Creating a Sustainable Digital Nomad Lifestyle
- Explored sustainability in the digital nomad lifestyle, balancing freedom and responsibility.
- Discussed eco-friendly travel, slow travel, and local involvement.
- Addressed personal well-being and community engagement.

Chapter 12: Future-Proofing Your Digital Nomad Lifestyle
- Focused on preparing for the future by embracing technological advancements, adapting to changing work trends, and promoting sustainability.
- Covered future-proofing financial success, staying agile and resilient, and building a supportive community.
- Emphasized the importance of adaptability, resilience, and a strong network.

These chapters provide a comprehensive guide for individuals seeking to lead a successful and fulfilling digital nomad lifestyle while thriving as entrepreneurs in the new economy. Whether you're a seasoned nomad or just starting your journey, these insights can help you navigate the challenges and opportunities that come with a location-independent lifestyle.

www.ingramcontent.com/pod-product-compliance
Lightning Source LLC
LaVergne TN
LVHW012128070526
838202LV00056B/5923